MARKETING by
DELIGHT

3/4/11

Roger,
Thanks for taking the
time to meet for coffee.
I loved your message
when I heard you
speak in Gig Harbor!
Hope you'll get a
nugget or three from
this! Your Pal,
Bob

MARKETING by
DELIGHT

Discover the fun way of
winning lifelong customers...

one nugget at a time

BOB *Island Boy* INGRAM
BRUCE *Coach* VOGT

Published by Advantage, Charleston, South Carolina.
Member of Advantage Media Group.

ADVANTAGE is a registered trademark and the
Advantage colophon is a trademark of Advantage Media Group, Inc.

Printed in the United States of America

ISBN: 978-1-59932-035-9

Library of Congress Control Number: 2007921313

TABLE OF CONTENTS

ACKNOWLEDGEMENTS

My inspiration and support has come from many people. My parents Ed and Emma Ingram provided me with the foundation to believe in myself. My wife Cara gave me an unbelievably great example of an extraordinary MBD marketer and was my sounding board throughout the writing phase. Sons Jason and Taylor keep me from taking myself too seriously! And, my dear friend Coach Bruce whose idea it was to write this book. He is the best co-author and partner a guy could ever have. Thank you all.

Bob Ingram

I dedicate this book to my wife Cathy and my three sons, Nathan, Bruce and Daniel they encouraged and yes even pushed me to put in writing the ideas expressed in this book. Cathy and my sons have lived with and listened to my lectures about the how much I love sales and salespeople. And how I wish I could reach every person involved in sales and marketing with the message of this book. They know that this book is from my heart.

Bruce Vogt

THANK YOU FOR BUYING OUR BOOK! We're confident you'll gain some marketing insight and inspiration. We believe we offer a different way of thinking about sales and marketing that will put more dollars in your pocket. Throughout **Marketing By Delight** (hereafter called MBD) we interchange the terms sales and marketing because we believe the lines blur in the real world every day. However, for the sake of simplicity we will use the term marketer when referring to a practitioner of sales or marketing.

Our book combines our sixty collective years of marketing experience in various industries and our goal is to help you expand your business through innovative marketing. We don't suggest that this is the end-all, beat-all of marketing books. No single book is. We do suggest you'll come away with new ideas and the seeds of many more.

It's a good idea to have a notepad handy as you read MBD. As you see applications for your business, make note of them for later reflection.

MBD is a concept that's more art than science but you *can* fine-tune your MBD skills. Much like learning to paint, some might have more aptitude but all can improve the skills they already bring to the table. We'll give you specific examples of MBD in the real world from our personal experiences as well as those told to us by fellow marketers and friends who gave us their true stories. From these stories and the philosophical view we share, you'll gain a new perspective in *your* marketing enabling you to integrate the data into your own business environment. We would never suggest that you totally adopt a MBD marketing style. It is best used as an adjunct to whatever proven marketing efforts are common within your industry. This is like having a new section in your playbook. The other sections are useful too, but MBD is the sizzle that can set you apart in the eyes of that most important person---your customer!

At the end of every chapter we give you golden marketing nuggets. Our definition of **marketing nugget** is any piece of information or wisdom which alone or when combined with other pieces is *useful* to the marketer. A nugget can be found anywhere, even in an otherwise boring presentation or typical situation. Look everywhere for nuggets, take them for what they are, and keep them in your arsenal. We've listed only the nuggets we've personally mined over the years. We haven't put them in any particular order of importance or any order at all. Some will strike a chord, and you'll see ways that particular nugget can be incorporated into something you already do *or* want to do. Others won't move you but that's okay. Some you may find silly, some you'll find insightful, and some you might say "Wow, I need to start doing that!" These nuggets are for you and we hope you'll take a few and drop them in your pocket for later use.

It's been a lot of fun writing this book. In the end, we believe we delivered on our goal to give the experienced *or* the novice marketer some useful information with which to go forth and multiply earnings. And definitely, have more fun doing it.

We hope you'll enjoy our book and find many useful nuggets to incorporate into your marketing strategy. We also invite you to visit our website at **www.marketingbydelight.com** to learn about our seminars, workshops, and other offerings. And, *please* share your MBD successes with us! We're already thinking about MBD II. Happy reading!

Your Marketing Pals,

Island Boy and Coach Bruce

MARKETING BY DELIGHT...
The Fun Way to Make Money

CHAPTER ONE

MBD IS A POWERFUL CONCEPT that evolved over the course of a couple of years as we watched several extraordinary marketers work their magic. And it may be something you're occasionally already doing without any conscious effort. If MBD is harnessed and *consistently* applied, it will put more money in your pocket.

Think about the word *delight* and what it conjures up. Maybe it's ***splashing*** in the ocean, ***running*** through a meadow, or ***hitting*** a homerun. Imagine giving your customers that level of delight. Do you think you'd "own" their business? You bet you would! The great news is that you *can* do this. You can create situations and opportunities for your customers to experience delightful moments thereby endearing them to you. You have the power to make them giggle, laugh, be amazed, surprised, or all four. Think creatively. **Have fun!**

There's a business owner in Maryland named Robert Schattner who built his company into a substantial small business generating about 15 million dollars in annual sales and employing over 100 people. Robert has outstanding, innate marketing instincts but doesn't want to be a full time marketer. He prefers to be a full time entrepreneur. His business is a franchise in the water/fire damage restoration field. He grew his company to be the largest, most successful franchisee in his system out of ninety-one. Robert always kept it simple while cutting right to the core of the business. One of his oft repeated adages is, "If you make people feel good, you're good." Robert understands the people side, the personal side of business—that if you make people feel good you'll do well. As he said about his business, "People don't care about how well you fix that wall. They expect that. What they care about is how you treat them."

As we began to study traits of successful marketers we started to see a certain commonality. Some were good practitioners of MBD without giving it conscious thought. One such marketer we'll call Susan had a knack for making people smile. She was "off the charts" good at bonding with customers personally and getting 'em to smile. She made them smile but didn't consistently tell her story about what her company offered. She'd get so sidetracked talking about personal stuff like kids, hobbies, etc., that she'd often forget to go over her company products and services. Yet she was *still* successful because she did one part of MBD so well... she made 'em smile. If only she knew when to make 'em smile and when to pivot and ask for the business. One needs to be a complete player whether in sports or business. We give the example of Susan only to illustrate that MBD is so powerful that a marketer can achieve decent success by using elements of it EVEN while lacking a complete understanding of all of its components. Imagine if you put it all together... how good would you be?

A couple of years ago, Island Boy was in charge of a charity golf tournament. All of the golfers were customers, insurance agents and adjusters who typically played a lot of tournaments, especially the "best ball" variety such as ours. So, to be different we dreamed up some surprises to **delight** our customers. After the golfers had all teed off and been on the course for about thirty minutes the funny business began. First, our professional impersonator arrived dressed just like Austin Powers. And your humble author donned a Hulk Hogan mask. Austin Powers and Hulk drove a golf cart around the course creating havoc, stopping to pose for pictures with the golfers. Austin had plenty of "Yeah, baby" and other lines he delighted the golfers with. Austin spent the afternoon with us and stayed for the evening banquet where he helped hand out trophies. We also had a 1940s cigarette girl making the rounds, handing out cigarettes and candy, and getting lots of attention. In the following weeks photos were delivered to each golfer....their picture with Austin Powers and Hulk. We had each photo in one of those plastic stands so they'd likely keep it in their office, a constant reminder of their day with us! Many did keep the picture displayed in their office. We had created a delightful experience for them and they didn't easily forget it.

The next year we continued the merriment with a Rodney Danger-field impersonator to the surprise our golfers. Rodney was escorted about the course by Rocky Balboa serving as his bodyguard. Again, all of this was a surprise to our guests and they were delighted as the following photos attest.

Rodney, Rocky, the cigarette girl, and friends.

Close-up of Cara the cigarette girl and Rocky "Island Boy" Balboa.

Another year our surprise guest was a Gomer Pyle impersonator who doubled as a golf trick shot artist. Before the tournament began he put on an amazing demonstration of trick shots using all kinds of clubs from 12' long to 18". He'd hit balls far and straight, left or right handed, blindfolded, standing backwards, it didn't matter. He was amazing! He did this with no hint of the Gomer Pyle within to be unveiled in a few hours. Later that evening, as the golfers were eating their meal and the awards beginning, Gomer Pyle, USMC, marched down the winding staircase toward the dining room in full dress uniform with the Marine Corps Anthem playing loudly. It was, as Gomer might have said, a hoot. Sha-Zamm! He had his impersonation down to a T and a went through a very nice routine. He had our guests howling. Some didn't even realize that Gomer and the golf pro, trick shot artist were one and the same.

But you don't need big events to delight people. You can do it every day in ways large and small. There are infinite ways. Keep a calendar of your customer's birthdays and send them unique, personalized cards that you obviously put thought into. It's good to get cards that allow you to insert your own handwritten punch lines. One savvy marketer uses a cartoon bubble above the head of the person in the photo and having him saying something funny. He recently sent a card that had a photo of a golfer lying on a green, pounding his fist on the grass as the ball teetered on the brink of the cup. He had a look of total frustration. In the cartoon bubble above his head the marketer wrote, "If *only* I could putt like Mike Watson." On the inside he wrote a birthday wish for Mike. As he reads that card Mike will have a moment of delight that he was remembered and got such a fun, personalized card.

An insurance agent on the West Coast takes digital photos of upscale homes he'd like to insure. He then uses computer software to make the photo look like a real oil painting. Next he puts the "oil painting" in a nice frame and mails it to the homeowner with his contact information and a note that says, "Your home is a work of art! Shouldn't it be insured like one"? Don't you think most homeowners are delighted to receive their "painting?" What a great idea! He's gained a number of new clients of the type he'd been seeking.

Brad Paisley, the country music singer, had a hit song called "Tiny Moments." The video features happy couples enjoying magical tiny moments in everyday life. The kind of moments we all live for IF we stop and enjoy them.

As the great marketer you are becoming, you'll be creating many tiny magical moments for your customers. And you'll enjoy the extra perks of having more fun on your job, having more friends, AND making more money.

We found a great example of MBD in the work of car salesman extraordinaire, German Vidal. German sells Hondas at a new car dealership in Bethesda, Maryland. German is among the top ten Honda salespersons in America. Originally from Bolivia he immigrated to this country and is a proud, naturalized citizen. His embrace of the American dream coupled with outstanding MBD skills have allowed German to achieve great success for himself and his family. Last year German sold 348 cars with his goal being to sell a car a day he points out that last year he had "17 days off and 365 minus 348 equals 17." German says that every sale has a golden moment. "The golden moment is when I give them the keys," he says. "The look on their faces—everyone is happy. A year from now, this brand new Accord will be sitting in the driveway of a brand new home. That's the picture I always have." Sometimes German does projects on his iMac for customers, unasked. He just finished a wedding album for a customer he recently met over a Civic deal. He sold a used car to another woman last year, and then learned her sister died. He made a DVD—"Remembering Nancy"—with snapshots, eulogies, music, and he presented twenty-five copies to the family! Nancy's sister wrote and said, "It was a gesture that will live forever in our family."

Minor league baseball teams have turned more and more to a MBD style of marketing to draw larger crowds and keep fans' interest once they are in the ball park. As lifelong baseball fans and attendees at many minor league games we can tell you that the minor leagues have embraced MBD marketing and it has helped boost minor league attendance across the country. Last year, minor league teams staged the following special events: *Nothing Night*: No concessions, no music, no announcers; *Bark in the park night*: Man's best friend admitted free; *Mullet Night*: Fans with mullets get in free, a mullet parade, and free haircuts. For in-game activities we discovered the following occurred at ball parks across America: *Hamster Ball Race*: Fans in costume race in giant hamster balls; *fan Velcroed to outfield wall for duration of game; llama races; midget wrestling; blindfolded cow tipping contest* with twelve-foot inflatable cow; and the long awaited *hairy back contest* with the grand prize a laser removal treatment.

MBD, in its most useful form, closely resembles a way of life, a way of being within the marketing world rather than a set of rigid rules to follow. In the MBD world creativity and positive thinking reign supreme, deeply rooted in the belief that all else will then fall into place. It's a way to think. MBD is art rather than science. And since art ability can be developed, so too can MBD skills.

So, how do you come up with good ideas to create these moments of delight? As you read through this book your eyes will be more open to opportunities. Awareness comes first and then the conscious decision to become an MBDer. Make it a part of your daily life to think about your customers. Think about their likes, what they are passionate about, and figure a way to delight them. You might "Google" their hobby, find an interesting article, and send it with a handwritten note. If you're reading this book you probably already work in marketing. So think about your current customers and which ones have hobbies or interests you're aware of. Maybe you have a customer who's a Disney nut and displays the Disney characters all over his or her office. One of your authors once had a customer who collected anything having to do with the Canadian Football League (CFL). Another collects golf balls with logos of colleges on them. There is no limit to the sometimes obscure, crazy stuff that we humans collect. If you've ever spent any time looking at the stuff people buy and sell on eBay you know this is true.

As you read our book you'll learn the key components in a good MBD oriented marketing plan. You'll then be well armed to go forth in the dog eat dog world of business and create your own MBD success stories.

Chapter Nuggets

Spread success credit to others: Always point to others who contributed to any success for which you're being lauded. We're reminded of the high ranking pilot who was shot down by enemy aircraft but parachuted to safety. Years later, by chance, he met the man who had actually packed that parachute. The moral of the story is…always remember that no matter how successful you are someone is packing your parachute. Give them credit!

Call someone by name the 2nd time you meet them: When you meet someone for the first time be sure to memorize their name so that you'll be able to immediately call them by their name when you see them the second time. Doing this the second time sends a big message that they made a good first impression upon you. This flatters the person and greatly increases the chances that they'll remember you and think well of you.

Support your customer's charities: When your customer asks you to support their charity, give something. You might be asked to purchase their daughter's Girl Scout cookies or to pledge money per mile for a walkathon. Your customer will remember that you supported them. If you don't, they'll remember that too!

Be ubiquitous: High visibility is a key to success. Go to industry meetings, advertise, attend events like golf tournaments, parties, etc.

Ask customers for advice: Whenever possible without being phony ask customers for advice. Most people feel flattered when others seek their counsel.

If you make 'em feel good, you're good: This quote came directly from Robert Schattner, a successful entrepreneur with whom your humble authors had the good fortune to work. Robert has a company that does major repairs to homes damaged by fire or flood. He always says customers don't care how well they repair the wall, they expect that to be done well. Rather, they care about how they were treated. Being treated well would mean good communication, courtesy, cleanliness, promptness, etc. Make 'em feel good and you are good (in their eyes).

Leave politics to the politicians: Steer clear of political discussions if possible. If you're positive that someone is of the same political bent as you are then it may serve as a good bonding thing but be very careful. Whichever side you're on roughly 50% of your customers are likely on the other side.

Sponsor educational seminars: If your industry requires people to attend continuing education seminars you need to sponsor them or put them on yourself. Most industries require re-certifications for various licenses and people are often scrambling at the last minute to find classes to meet their requirements. They'll be very grateful to you for providing the class and will, of course, favor you with their business. One marketer we know held a four hour morning classes at the Outback Steakhouse followed by lunch . The marketer asked the restaurant manager if he'd open in the morning and let him teach a class if he guaranteed forty people for lunch. The manager said yes and the marketer has held many classes there over the years. Each class with lunch costs about $1,000 which is paid for many times over from the business sent by the grateful attendees.

Have something in your briefcase to amuse kids: It is not an uncommon occurrence on sales calls to find that your customer has their child in the office with them. Maybe school's out that day or the child is with the parent for another reason. Your customer will be **delighted** at any attention you give their child. Think in terms of having a couple of cheap pairs of funny glasses or a coloring book—something that that you can give the child. He or she will tell their mom or dad about the nice man or woman who gave him/her a present. Great PR for you!

Befriend the gatekeeper: The receptionist or "gatekeeper" is a powerful person. This person can also be a tremendous ally and helpful to you. He or she has the power to let you in *or* keep you out. Your wonderful presentation filled with MBD moments won't do you a bit of good if you can't get past the gatekeeper.

Make leaps of trust: You can get to know people quicker if you *choose* to give them the trust that normally would come from knowing them longer. You have to trust your gut to a large degree with this. If you truly have bad vibes about someone don't give them the trust we're discussing here. We're talking about times when you have a good feeling about the person. There is, after all, much more good than bad in most people. So, go ahead, open up and trust more freely. You'll build more and richer relationships.

Money is your friend: At first this may sound strange but we believe that it is helpful to cultivate (in your mind) a relationship with money. Rather than viewing money as a necessary evil and the source of corruption as some do, we ask you to start looking upon money as your friend. Pick up coins you find and as you drop them into your pocket say, "Money is my friend." One of your humble authors began doing this several years ago and his income skyrocketed in the next few years. It's good karma, man!

Express gratitude often: Tell your customers often that you appreciate them and look them in the eye when you say it.

Mail stuff in unusual ways: Did you know that you can mail almost anything as long as it's not breakable? Travel agent Anita Pagliasso-Balamane said she once mailed out invitations for a baby shower in actual plastic baby bottles with confetti inside. It was under a buck to send each one and she got a great response. She delighted them! She also tells of the time she mailed a "coconut" postcard to a client. It was an actual coconut with a thank you note pained on it. You may not want to get as "off the beaten path" as mailing coconut postcards but at least think about unusually shaped envelops and boxes. Make your mail stand out, whether it's one piece or an entire direct-mail campaign.

CHAPTER TWO

Building Your Personal Image

CHAPTER TWO

A GREAT PERSONAL IMAGE IS CRUCIAL to successful *Marketing By Delight*. Sometimes, you'll hear people say, "so and so has *it*." "It" usually is that intangible, hard to describe but discernable aura or presence that successful people have. We believe this intangible quality is closely connected to one's image. And image can be consciously altered, for better or worse.

There's a great story about Ben Franklin which provides an example of cultivating one's image. Consider how enterprising the young Ben Franklin was as he was building a career as a printer and publisher in the nascent city of Philadelphia: Franklin was a newcomer to this town of 4,000 and looking for fame and fortune. He wanted to get noticed and noticed quickly. And, he rarely missed an opportunity. Franklin wasn't the type of young man to wait for things to happen. As the publisher and owner of the up and coming Philadelphia Gazette young Franklin needed lots of paper. So he turned a mundane paper delivery into a marketing opportunity. Rather than have the stock paper delivered to his shop, Ben arranged to meet the delivery man on the edge of town where he loaded the paper into his wheelbarrow. The delivery occurred at the peak of the hustle bustle of young, vibrant Philadelphia. It was the rush hour of their day. Ben proceeded to briskly and purposely push his wheelbarrow through the crowd as though rushing to important work. He even managed to adjust the wheel to create a noticeable squeak when he pushed it through the busy town square, thus getting more heads turning his way. People saw him and couldn't help but have an image of a very industrious young man destined for success. Perfect, just what he had wanted them to think. And it wasn't phony. He wasn't conning anyone. He just presented himself in such a way to allow his true inner self to shine through. He *was* ambitious and he *was* destined for success.

So are you!

And you can find situations in your world to forge the image *you* want to portray. It might involve heading a committee to gain visibility within your industry. It could involve a million things. Nobody can give you a list—you have to have the mindset to look for them, as Franklin did. They're all around you, every day.

A modern day example of image creation is illustrated by a woman named Cara who represents Portland, Oregon in Washington, D.C. She is a marketer extraordinaire. Cara's goal is to bring convention business to Portland and she's *very* successful. She markets to the various industry associations based in Washington, D.C. all of whom hold annual conventions. There are over 1,000 associations she markets to and she has managed to get noticed in ways even Mr. Franklin would have admired.

One of the larger associations, a society of scientists and engineers, has an annual convention. Cara and her co-marketer, Colleen, always sponsor the coffee breaks which are *far* from the usual coffee breaks. One of their

"Lucy and Ethel" stomping grapes and dazzling customers.

memorable breaks created quite a buzz. As the attendees came out of their meeting, heading to the coffee table, they saw Cara and Colleen dressed as Lucy and Ethel stomping grapes to make wine. That's, of course, one of the classic scenes from the old I Love Lucy television show. Most of the attendees grew up watching the show, remembered the episode, and loved the re-enactment. The "actresses" never broke character and played their skit to the hilt. They replicated the attire of Lucy and Ethel and had a poster of the real scene nearby. Do you think those customers and prospects will remember Cara and Colleen? Would just a sign saying, "Sponsored by Portland" gotten much, if any attention?

*Right after 9/11 Cara and Colleen delighted customers with their
Uncle Sam and Betsy Ross patriotic attire. They posed for photo after photo with
their friends and customers as competitors turned green with envy.*

Over the years, Cara and Colleen have built such a reputation for their imaginative, fun coffees breaks that the stuffed shirt scientists usually come flying out of their meetings and practically sprint to them! This is a great example of *Marketing By Delight*. Some of the attendees in the above example are old customers with whom a relationship is already established and some are "newbies." Cara easily moves into a more meaningful dialogue with customers after having fun experiences with them after they've seen her in a different light. She's more interesting and real and they easily relate to her. And, she has created an **image** as a marketer who is fun and interesting, and maybe a bit quirky but in a good way. The technique they used is a variation on the one used by Ben Franklin with his squeaky wheelbarrow over 200 years ago. Once the ice is broken, Cara builds a RELATIONSHIP with the customer, which greatly increases her chances of a booking for the city she markets. As long as the marketer can successfully pivot to getting serious about closing the sale these out-of-the-box, attention-getting episodes can help you leapfrog over your competitors in the battle to get your prospect thinking about YOU rather than the competitor! Remember, you're battling for "airtime" in your customer's minds.

By the way, it's good to remember that the marketing techniques discussed in these pages are applicable to virtually any business or marketing endeavor. Certainly, it's true of this concept of creating the image you want and need to be successful.

Your customer begins forming an image of you **before** you have time to establish your credibility *or* your company's. First, you're judged by your dress. So, how *do* you dress? Our rule of thumb is simple and has served us well over the years… **dress *slightly* better than those you are calling upon**. Remember also, to factor in regional differences if you're covering a diverse territory. Many marketers cover multiple states and regions and you must adjust to the differences. *Always* adjust to the customer if there's not a big downside to doing so.

In some marketing jobs you cover a territory and make the rounds to your customers on a regular schedule. An outstanding manager of one such marketer once said to remember that the customers only saw him (the marketer) four times a year and therefore it was crucial to be "on" and always have a productive, positive visit. As a marketer your latest visit will essentially be your customers' memory of you for the next three months, so make it a good one. We suggest you view your sales calls almost like a play or skit and make sure you're "on." Even if you are feeling like you don't have your "A" game on a given day you can still rise to the occasion by imagining you're doing a 15-20 minute skit—the show must go on!

A big part of image is to be seen as a positive, upbeat, can-do, keep your word, kind of person. It's important to project this EVERY TIME. If you're feeling down you may have to fake it on a given day or two. You just have to do that sometimes. It isn't easy to operate near optimal level all the time. If it were, anybody could do it and you wouldn't have the chance to make the big bucks. If you expect to have an occasional down time, and have a plan for getting through it, you'll have a big advantage. As a long time friend of the authors says, "appreciate the valleys because without them you wouldn't know the joy of the peaks." Relish the difficult times because your competitor has them too. Who deals with them better? It's a bit like running a marathon, everybody prefers running on flat ground or downhill but races are won and lost on the tough parts, the hills.

In cycling, Lance Armstrong dominates on the toughest hills. As a marketer when it's tough going, you have to stay positive and continue to portray yourself as though you're on top of the world! And look to those hills... opportunity lies there waiting for you.

 Here's some practical advice you won't get in most sales training. Be very aware that you may be watched when you least expect it. No, it's not the government. It's your customer. When driving to an appointment smart marketers get into their role prior to even arriving in the area surrounding the office or meeting place. Many marketers don't think about the fact that buildings actually have windows! Consider the otherwise great marketer who drives fast and recklessly into their prospects parking lot only to have the person he's coming to call upon watching out his office window. Or worse yet, almost collide with your prospect in the parking lot. Yes, a customer can form a negative image of you before you even meet him. On the contrary, you can begin to foster a positive image too. Always make it a point to quickly get out of your car and walk briskly and enthusiastically toward your meeting place.

Assume you're being watched. The image you can create if you're being watched is one of a marketer who is looking forward to the meeting and enthused about it. And ready! And it helps you to get into the positive mindset you'll need throughout the meeting. Plus, you never know who you might meet in the lobby, the elevator, on the stairs, or outside the building. Hold the door for them, be polite to everyone. The person you held the door for may be the number two person at the company who is called into your meeting and you have already established a positive image of yourself with that person! Of course, the same holds true with leaving the building and surrounding area. Assume you're being watched as you leave too. Whether or not you had a successful sales call always leave in the same positive manner as when you arrived. After all, if you didn't make the sale this time you got closer or you know to move onto the next prospect... either way a positive result.

One last comment about image: in many cases the marketer is the only person in the company actually known to the customer. You ARE the company in their minds. That's why it's so important to build a positive image.

Chapter Nuggets

Label yourself as you want to be: Give yourself whatever label you aspire to, before you achieve it. By defining yourself clearly, you will gravitate to that image. This doesn't need to be broadcast to the world. It's best kept to yourself and used as your own secret motivator. For instance, this is our first book but we viewed ourselves as authors long before we even started it. This sounds corny but it works.

Be early: Always get to your meetings early. Factor in extra time for traffic problems or other potential delays that could cause you to be late. You may even have to drive around the block or stop for a cup of coffee nearby to kill a few minutes but that's okay. It gives you time to relax and focus on your upcoming meeting. Arriving late to meetings often changes the whole dynamics, usually not in your favor, because your meeting is getting too close time-wise to his next one. Being late, except for the rare circumstance that can derail even the best made early arrival plans, can begin your meeting on a weak note.

Be obsessive about numbers: Coach Bruce and Island Boy shout it from the mountaintops… it's all about the numbers! Figure out how many calls you need to make to have the number of sales you'll need to hit your income goal. Know what that number is on a weekly basis. Become obsessed about making that many calls each week. Don't stop until you do.

When possible keep your presentation to twenty minutes: It seems to us that attention spans are getting shorter and shorter. If you can shorten up your basic presentation and make it move along quicker with power you'll have the best chance for success.

Say these five magic words often… I'll take care of it: Be known as the person at your company who speaks up and says, *"I'll take care of it"* when something needs to get done. And then follow through. If things ever get rough at your company the people who take care of things are the ones who survive and eventually prosper.

Be first: Be the first in your industry to do something a certain way. In America, the person who comes in second is usually forgotten while people who do things first are idolized. Do you know who the *second* woman was to fly across the Atlantic? The second man to walk on the moon? Get your competitors chasing you and your ideas! Be first and be remembered.

Buy specialty advertising items with long shelf lives (staying power): Invest in only those promotional items which are have long shelf lives or staying power... as in "staying" in front of your customer. Coffee mugs, magnets, mouse pads.

Have an upbeat phone message: This seems obvious but we know some great upbeat marketers who have plain vanilla phone messages. Put some pizzazz into it and remember that this is yet another chance to convey a message to your customer. You may say something to pique their interest in one of your services or products. A good rule of thumb is to review your message on the 1st of each month and ask yourself if there is something new you're promoting that you'd like to include. Remember though, to keep it short. People don't want to listen to an extended commercial. It's also a good idea to ask someone whose opinion you value to give you feedback on how your message comes across.

Get free publicity, send press releases: Did you know the majority of stories in newspapers are there because someone sent a press release? It's true. The trick is to make sure yours stands out. The keys are: An enticing subject line that gets to the point quickly, don't use attachments if e-mailing. Always include a link to your Web site, don't take no or no responses personally, make it newsworthy, and don't make it about me, me, me. Make sure your writing is clear about the benefits provided by your info, and make sure the first paragraph contains the power.

Put your photo in all ads: If you run an ad consider using your photo. Some people are not comfortable doing this but it is a fact that a person's photo in an ad makes the ad more noticeable. The authors have experienced this ourselves and have seen how much more effective and memorable ads with photos are. You may even want to consider adding some humor. We've had great success using cartoon bubbles over our heads in the photo to impart our message.

Wear your family on your sleeve: We refer to this as the Jim Mizell rule. Jim was a marketing rep for an insurance company in Washington, D.C. He worked on the wholesale side of the business and marketed to insurance agents. Many of the people he called on were women. Jim is happily married with two young adorable children and loved to talk with his customers about *their* families. Of course, they'd then ask about Jim's and out would come the pictures. Bingo! He bonded with them right there. His manager finally understood how effective this was when one of Jim's customers asked him... "Do you know why we LOVE Jim Mizell?" The manager said, "no, why?" She said, "because he's such a great family man. He's always showing us pictures of his wife and kids." The key was that Jim is very sincere and always showed great interest in *their* families too. Jim is genuine. He wouldn't have elicited such a positive reaction if he'd been self centered when showing his customer his family photos.

Become known for an event and create a tradition: Some great marketers we've known have become well known within their industries for events. For instance, a sharp marketing rep. of Safelite Auto Glass each year holds a monster crab feast for people (insurance agents and body shops) who send him business. This has grown to be a much anticipated event and people want to be on the invite list. They know, though, that invites go only to those people using the company. A marketer for another company has a blow-out Halloween party each year. Yet another marketer charters a bus to take groups to events and the bus ride provides an excellent setting for jocularity. Whatever you decide to do, make it fun! These types of events give you unmatched opportunities to bond with your customers in ways you'd never be able to in the normal work environment.

Wear something memorable: Unique ties, scarves, or jewelry. They make great ice breakers.

Submit articles: Submit articles or a letter to the editor of your industry trade publication.

MBD High Espionage

CHAPTER THREE

WHETHER WE CONSCIOUSLY THINK OF IT OR NOT, we are all in the info gathering business in our business *and* personal lives. We do it naturally. As a marketer you *have* to do it **well** if you want to reach your potential as an MBD marketer. Detailed info about your customer gives you the perspective on him or her to choose your MBD route. Some people are better than others at gathering info but it *is* a skill that can be developed. This chapter will give you some very specific ways to obtain information about your customer and that will lead to more money in your pocket!

The first essential is to use a PDA to store and sort customer data. It should be small and carried just about everywhere you go. Think of it as buying about a trillion megabytes of memory for your brain. It can simplify your life and make you money. Hmmm… that could be useful, couldn't it?

Several years ago a friend and fellow marketer told me his colleagues laughed at his 3 by 5 card filing system he carried around everywhere. His 3 by 5 cards had dog-eared corners and the business cards stapled on them. It wasn't pretty but it was "his system." He was comfortable with it but it was starting to get unwieldy. It had to go! So with a heavy heart he purchased his first Palm Pilot and started to enter customer info. Whenever he needed to look at a particular 3 by 5 card he'd enter that info into his PDA and threw away the card with great ceremony! It took about nine months to go through them all but it was well worth the effort. He did a few conversions a day and it didn't seem so daunting. **Now**, before this marketer goes to his customer's office, he checks his PDA for notes from previous visits to help find common ground on which to bond. Why care about bonding? **It ultimately puts money in your pocket**! Suppose that Mabel the receptionist told the marketer that her grandson is playing in the Little League Championship on July 4th and he made that note in his PDA. Imagine how *delighted* Mabel will be when he walks through the door in August with a smile and says, "Hi Mabel, how'd your grandson do in that championship game?"

Do you think he'll have any problems getting through that gatekeeper? Or that maybe he might get a helpful heads-up sometime? Befriend the receptionist! That's just one example of a good use of a PDA. Consider the following list of some real life uses of PDA's, which have benefited marketers and allowed them to be much more successful. And remember, these are just a few examples. You will dream up others unique to your contacts, goals, and overall sales environment. Imagine that you have 2,000 contacts with good "Intel" on each one. Remember that the key is to put in lots of info about your customer. Whatever you learn from a visit, phone call, or e-mail should be entered into your PDA within a few minutes. Consider some of the following examples of uses:

- A marketer in Georgia sorted out his customers who are baseball fans and put together an invite list to take a group out to a minor league baseball game. It was a huge hit and by using his PDA he was assured of not forgetting anyone.

- You can search for and come up with a list of all customers on a certain street, in a certain town, or state. This is very helpful when making calls and wanting to be sure you won't miss someone in the geographic area you're working.

- You'll be able to search for any group within your contact database with a common interest such as art lovers, dog owners, avid readers, etc. You are then able to send interesting articles to a number of customers about their particular interest along with a nice, handwritten note. Do you think many of your competitors do that? Maybe they won't read this book.

- You can make cross references, i.e., when you learn that one of your contacts knows another, make notes in each file. Then you're reminded when you review the notes before your sales call. Often you'll be able to capitalize by telling one contact that you and his friend do business together. Your credibility gets an automatic upward spike! It's almost like a referral except in this case *you* created it, by gathering info!

- And, you can use the memo section to create lists of people who may want to be reminded of certain things. It may be an upcoming industry related continuing education course. Use your imagination to help your contacts in as many ways as possible. They'll be delighted that you thought of them.

The examples above represent just a small sampling of the many ways a PDA can help you grow your business but it IS just a machine, a tool. You do the real work with your great marketing skills. And information gathering is the foundation of it all. One of the best info gathering techniques is **Office Reading**. Throw off the shackles of illiteracy and learn to Office Read! Reading an office is being observant about "things" when visiting a customer in his office, learning from your observations, and using that knowledge to strengthen the relationship. Of course, you don't want to be too obvious, so be cool and subtle about it. Most offices contain lots of clues about what is important to that person. Their personal space is usually adorned with photos, diplomas, keepsakes, trinkets, decorations, plants, books, and so on. Ask about some of the things you see. Most people enjoy talking about themselves and their interests. If you see something in their office that indicates you have a common interest you've hit pay dirt because you've found some common ground. By "reading an office" you'll find customers who enjoy the same authors you do, root for the same teams, own the same breed of dog, or have children who play the same instrument as your child. Make it fun. Challenge yourself. See if you can learn five or more things about someone by reading their office. We suggest you think of the 3L's: Look, Listen, and Learn. You'll note that the 3L's don't have a T. They say nothing about talking. As Grandma used to say, "You have two ears and only one mouth for a reason!"

LOOK, LISTEN, AND LEARN

When you do talk, do so in a manner to draw your customer out. Ask open ended questions about those things you've gleaned from "reading" their office or them. People love to talk about themselves… its human nature.

We'll give you some specific techniques you can practice and become proficient at to help get your customer to open up to you. Sometimes you can get the customer to reveal something about himself, if you begin by telling something about you. Choose something non-controversial and not too heavy duty that would cause the customer to think you are inappropriate given that it's early in the relationship. You might potentially offend the customer. You can also use a technique called body mirroring. Your customer may be pressed forward looking tense and you notice that you too, are leaning forward. Lean back in your seat and adopt a more relaxed posture and often the customer will mirror you without even realizing it. Thus, he actually does relax a bit by having a different posture. Conversely, if you want him to pay closer attention you might lean forward. He will most likely lean forward too. Try this a few times, just for fun.

One of the gurus of information gathering for marketers is a gentleman from Minnesota by the name of Harvey MacKay. MacKay owns an envelop company which bears his name and is the dominant player within their marketing territory. His book, *How to Swim with the Sharks Without Being Eaten Alive*, explains the great lengths to which McKay Envelope marketers go to gather info on their customers. They **really** get to know them. McKay reasoned that an envelop is an envelop, is an envelop. There are no substantial differences between his physical product and that of his competitors. He decided that GREAT marketing rooted in information gathering would be his key to dominance. He then developed his visionary system of great marketing. MacKay marketers "bought into" the system and became so bonded with McKay customers that business soared. They kept detailed records of "Intel" they picked up in sales calls. With each sales call the "Intel" got better and more detailed. After a while, since the sales rep knew what made his customers tick, subsequently they bonded with them. At this point, the customer crossed a line and usually thought of their reps. as a friend, not *just* a marketer.

With this type of relationship the customer will be open to giving you business and will prefer to do business with you rather than your competitor. They will WANT to give you business!

But wait a minute, isn't there more to it? Yes! You have to care, *really* care about your customer as a person, as a fellow human being. And you can't fake caring. People have built in BS detectors. Develop a more caring attitude about everyone whose path you cross. Think about this one: How do you treat people from whom you can derive no benefit? Do you treat the toll taker as well as the banker? How about the stranger in the doctor's waiting room? Baseball Hall of Fame manager Sparky Anderson once said that if he went out to dinner with someone who was rude to the server, he would not go to dinner with that person again. Be nice to everyone. It's a lot easier than trying to pick and choose… you won't guess wrong! Applying this path of logic to marketing calls you want to be sure to be nice to everyone you call on within an organization starting with the receptionist. Meet as many people within an organization as you can and commit their names to memory. Then watch the look on their face when you say hello to them by name when you meet them for just the second time. Then they'll remember **you** for having remembered **them**! And you'll start to be viewed within their organization as someone who is pretty sharp. You never know who the players are within a company or who influences whom, so impress them all…. create that great image discussed in chapter two. Often you can work your way up within an organization by first making progress with some lower ranking or mid- ranking people who in turn help you get to the decision makers. When you *do* meet the Big Cheese you may be able to reference one of the staff by name which may lead to some "Intel" about that person's role. Bingo! Right into your PDA!

Chapter Nuggets

Form a "Junta" or Brain Trust: Ben Franklin formed a group of intellectuals who met regularly to discuss issues of their times and come up with solutions. He called his group the Junta and it remained intact for decades. You can adopt a variation on this theme by forming a group of marketers you respect. Make sure they aren't competitors or friends of competitors. They should be in somewhat related areas so that members at least understand the basics of other members businesses. Meetings can be held at restaurants or can rotate between members' homes.

Beware of the Robert who doesn't like to be called Bob: You can never tell if someone likes to go by their formal name or the nickname. Some people have a real dislike for one or the other. What's the safest course of action? Just ask.

Stretch geographic limits: If you're a commissioned marketer and can make more money if your company broadens it's territory then lobby for that. Maybe you can service the adjacent county or state.

Exercise regularly for high energy levels: A great marketer needs to be in good health. You probably have heard that exercise increases one's metabolism and energy level. A high energy level is needed by just about everyone in our fast paced world but especially hard working marketers striving to be the best they can be.

Outwork your competitors: You won't beat your competitors every day but vow to be more consistent and persistent over time. Beat them in the long run. Consistency and persistency are more important than intensity. View it as a marathon rather than a sprint.

Namedrop: It shortens the acceptance time in the bonding/friendship process if your customer knows that a friend of his is also a friend of yours. The assumption is that is you're good enough to have earned friendship with my friend then you must be ok.

Learn to do stuff others don't know how to do: As a very young man just entering marketing a grizzled veteran marketer told Island Boy to find things at his company to do that nobody else wanted to do or could do. He said it'd be job security and it's a good thing to think about once in a while. Think about it… if anyone could do what you do there's no incentive to keep you around!

Allow yourself to get on a roll: As a marketer try to keep large blocks of time available to market your product or service. This allows you to get on a roll with your marketing energy. It's very difficult to market for an hour or two, do some paperwork, and then market some more. You lose psychological momentum from starting, stopping, and them starting again. It's easy to get caught up in stopping by your office to pick up a thing or two but beware the trap. Invariably, people will ask you things, you'll see some mail to look at or something else will cause you to be in your office much longer than you thought you'd be. Guard your marketing time… it's too valuable to waste.

Become a great networker: Great networkers never take a day off… they're always networking. People who network well understand that it is more about farming than hunting. Networking is about cultivating relationships. According to Ivan Misner who is the CEO and founder of BNI, the world's largest networking organization some of the key traits of successful networkers are: **following up on referrals, a positive attitude, enthusiasm, trustworthiness, good listening skills, thanking people, sincerity, and enjoying helping others.** All of these traits tie in with building and maintaining relationships which is discussed throughout MBD.

Market in bad weather: Make a special effort to market even harder in lousy weather. As marketers, Coach Bruce and Island Boy always found that competitors tend to slack off on bad weather days. Also, it's a good conversation starter. This works well for "drop in" marketing calls. People usually will ask why you're out on such a lousy day. There are all kinds of answers. Two we like are: "I wanted to see you and wasn't going to let the weather stop me" or "I know my competitors aren't out today!"

Repeat yourself: The fact that you've told your customer about your other services doesn't mean they'll remember. In the information age we live in a person has enough of a challenge remembering all they need to about their own business, much less yours. So, keep telling them.

CHAPTER FOUR

A Hidden MBD Opportunity

CHAPTER FOUR

THERE IS ONE GROUP THAT SOME MARKETERS IGNORE yet the highly successful marketers know better! What is this almost always overlooked marketing opportunity and why is it important? It's your OWN COMPANY! If you understand and incorporate this concept into your marketing you'll have a leg up on your competitors. If you're starting to buy into the power of the whole MBD concept imagine the impact if your entire organization "gets it."

All truly great sales and marketing people not only do an over-the-top job promoting their company externally but they do so internally as well. This is important for a number of reasons. **Every** interaction between your customer and your company creates an impression, an image of your organization. It's crucial that everyone in the company know and understand this. And, it's up to you to lead the way. Remind your co-workers that you ALL work in marketing! Yes, that means your accounting department, production, the receptionist, and your IT department. Think about all of the times that your customers talk with someone at your company other than you. Each of these interactions is an opportunity. Does your company make the most of these opportunities? Or are they oblivious? Probably they are somewhere in between. Customers make judgments based on how they are received and treated. They make these judgments with every interaction. Do some of your co-workers view the customer as an interruption to his or her work? Or as an opportunity to show how much they appreciate them? Will your co-worker treat the customer with the same high level of appreciation and commitment that you do? Who answers the phone at your company? Do they sound enthused and make the caller feel welcomed?

We know an outstanding receptionist who has a sign on her desk which reads, "Director of First Impressions." She makes a great first impression for her company whether it is in person or when answering the phone. Clearly, she understands how vital her role is to the overall operation and that she works in marketing.

Make it your job to be sure that everyone understands about these opportunities and that how your customer is treated should be congruent with the message you're delivering in the field. You're out there promoting your fine company… you need to be sure that your company is coming across that way. We recommend sitting down with the president or owner of your company and express your beliefs about how vital it is for everyone at the company to buy into the "we're all in marketing' concept. Ask for his support and be ready with suggestions on how to implement this thinking at your company. If the BC (Big Cheese) is willing to have a company-wide meeting to emphasize this then the message will be strongly delivered, and hopefully well received. A meeting can be followed by periodic reminders either via memos, e-mails, pay check stuffers or whatever else you can come up with. Certainly it should be mentioned at subsequent meetings which focus on other issues. In this way it will gradually become a part of the company culture. And, it's always good to recognize in some way those people who do "get it" and embrace this concept. If the top managers and the BC don't buy into it you might think about dusting off your resume!

As a marketer you will often need the help of others within your company to deliver on promises to customers. Perhaps the company can score big points if a shipment is delivered a couple of days early. To do so, you may need the full support and understanding of the production manager or another department head. There may be times when your accounts receivable department inadvertently turns off a long term customer by sending out a late notice when a more diplomatic approach might be called for. You need to have a good relationship with everyone so that they are likely to give you a "heads-up" on sensitive customer issues. Many a marketing rep has been sabotaged from within because he or she has failed to cultivate good relationships with your co-workers.

How do you build and maintain great internal relationships? First, don't be a marketing snob! Face it; other departments sometimes view marketers as prima donnas. In their minds we're the lucky ones who have freer, more flexible schedules, expense accounts, and free lunches. They sometimes think that we're over-appreciated while they feel under-appreciated. The way to combat this is to be especially careful to give everyone their proper amount of respect and appreciation. When you get compliments about a fellow employee from one of your customers make sure to share that compliment with the employee and management. It makes it a lot easier to bring back a complaint if everyone knows you also proudly bring back the compliments. Go out of your way to cultivate friendships across department lines. You may occasionally do something fun and informal across departmental lines like going bowling or to shoot pool. You then become more than just the marketing person. It gets back to what Sparky Anderson espouses as discussed in the last chapter. Be nice to everyone. It doesn't cost you a thing and it enriches your life. Remember too, that every department contributes to the success of the overall organization. You can't possibly do without them. Fortunately, they need you too. So, throw off the shackles of cross departmental rivalries and jealously.

Ideally, each person views people in other departments as internal customers and works to please them. For instance, if the marketing department wants to know how sales are trending in certain geographic areas they might look to the IT Department as the provider of a report showing that breakdown. Hopefully, the IT folks will view the marketers as internal customers and get the info to them as quickly as possible *and* with a smile. Be the catalyst at your company to bring departments together. And always be optimistic about your company even if you're going through rough times. Others look to you for direction. **Marketers are expected to be leaders!**

Look for opportunities to pitch in and help co-workers unexpectedly, especially when it's "not your job." Like the bumper sticker says, "practice random acts of kindness"… within your own company. You'll garner a lot of respect and appreciation and your co-workers will be willing to run through walls for you when you're really in a pinch and need *their* help. And take the time to actually talk to your peers about how things are in their world. Just ask. Take a **sincere** interest and do the same thing you do with customers… ask open ended questions and be a good listener.

You may start out doing some of these things because they'll ultimately put more money in your pocket but it won't work *as well* if it's strictly done for money. What's likely to happen is that by becoming a leader internally as discussed in this chapter you'll find your job more fun, more satisfying, and ***then...*** the money will flow. Something done for the right reasons almost always brings the better result.

Chapter Nuggets

Have your meeting in cool places: If you're in charge of renting meeting space to meet with clients/prospects consider going to usual places instead of meeting hall B at the Holiday Inn! One MBD marketer we know had a meeting at an historic home in Washington D.C. that used to be the home of a prominent brewery owner during the FDR presidency. The group had their business meeting but left absolutely delighted by the official tour they were given and a catered lunch. You'll never be able to go back to the Holiday Inn… your customers will expect you to do it again but that's a nice problem to have. And it ensures that your meetings will be well attended.

To make a friend, be a friend: Go first! Be a friend first. The other person will usually follow suit.

Talk about books: Most people in the United States read, and fiction novels seem to top the list. So many people have their favorite genres or authors. In you know your customer reads engage him/her in a discussion about the types of books they like to read. If they like some of the same type of book that you do you'd be able to loan them one of your favorites that they haven't read yet. We've made friends with customers through bonding over books.

Give your time wisely: Your time is the most precious gift you can give anyone. Be wise with it. Give freely of it to those you care most deeply about but save some for strangers too. The strangers are new friends you haven't met yet.

Success or failure: nearly right vs. exactly right: The difference between success and failure is often very small. Sometimes, it's like the difference between nearly right and exactly right. If you're nearly right you're almost there. Keep going.

Welcome solicitors: How many marketers reading this have "no soliciting" signs on your office door? We bet that most of you do. It's amazing when you think about it. Almost every insurance office we've ever visited has one… yet they themselves are the ultimate solicitors. One rebel agent we know put tape over the "no" so that the sign outside his door just read "soliciting." Why not welcome solicitors, let them in. Three things can happen and two of them are good. You can like what they're selling and buy, you might see a new marketing twist, or you might not like any part of the experience. They may know someone who needs your services or product. Network with them.

Write plans: They don't have to be fancy plans or for anyone else to see, just write things down that you want to accomplish. The more you write things down the deeper the desire is implanted in you to do that thing.

The 30 minute blitz: You may not be so fortunate as to be able to devote all or most of your time to marketing. If your situation is such that you have to find marketing time in bits and pieces during the in- between times of your other duties consider the 30 minute blitz. Use a timer so that you won't have to keep looking at your watch. Your "blitz" might be to call old or current customers to ask for referrals or to hand write postcards to key prospects. How you decide to spend your marketing 30 minute blitz is not as important as scheduling it regularly.

Consider hiring interns for marketing help: Your local college or university probably has business or marketing interns looking to hook up with companies like yours where they can earn college credits for being an intern. It doesn't hurt to call and ask. An intern may be able to help with a wide variety of things. One such example is developing your website. Some interns will work without pay although others will expect at least some monetary compensation.

Save at least 10% of what you earn: Build wealth by living beneath your means and investing regularly. Set it up to be automatic done. Pay yourself before everybody else!

Pass out sticky pads: Everyone loves and uses these. We're talking about the 4 by 4 post-it pads. Of course your name, phone number, and website address should be on all sides thereby clearly visible on a desk. The 4 by 4's last a very long time and people will be panicking when they start to run out. We suggest you take extra time to write 2 or 3 "secret" messages on random sheets within the cube. Weeks later your customer will tear a post-it and see your brilliant marketing message written on the next one. You'll surprise and probably delight them.

Send cards on odd holidays: Look up the off the wall holidays and have some fun. For instance, August 21st is Hawaii Admissions Day which celebrates Hawaiian statehood. Send a lei to your customers with a Hawaiian postcard containing your irresistible marketing message. And find an unusual package to send it in. Send a card with a Husky dog on March 4th, the day the Iditarod starts. Write a note telling your customer/prospect that these are the hardest working dogs in the world and that you'll work equally hard to earn and keep their business.

Have meetings at unusual times: Instead of asking for a 2 o'clock meeting ask to meet at 2:07. It'll be remembered.

The harder you work the luckier you get: This is an old one but is so true that it had to be included as one of our nuggets.

You can learn almost anything in 15 minutes a day: Scholars in the science of learning tell us that we can better master a subject by studying daily for a short period of time. You retain much more than you would by studying once a week for a longer time. If you're thinking of learning something new but hesitant due to thinking it'd take too much time then this nugget may be just what the doctor ordered to get you going!

Don't try to do too much: Successful marketers know that if you try to chase two rabbits you aren't likely to catch either one. Choose your priorities and be single minded about pursuing them.

Keep doing what works: Marketers are natural tinkerers, with ideas. We like to try new things and we get bored easily. Resist the urge to do a lot of tinkering with things that work.

Give movie tickets away as a thank you: Most people like to go to a movie or have friends and family who do. A couple of movie tickets have proved to be an excellent inducer of referrals for one marketer who buys them in bulk from Loew's Theatre.

Sponsor holes at charity golf tournaments: Charity golf tournaments are big and you should be very visible at those attended by your target market. But don't just sponsor a hole, make a bigger splash. We've sponsored Hole-In –One Contests which pays $25,000 if someone hits a hole-in-one. We get this insured and pay the insurance company about $400 and they pay the 25k if someone does ace the hole. Or have a car as the prize! One MBD marketer we know has a "marshmallow driving contest" set up on the course. The golfer driving a marshmallow the farthest wins a great prize… usually a television. Our marketer friend is tired of doing the same thing every year by can't give it up because everyone looks so forward to it. What a problem!

Make friends, sales follow: Make friends with people. Most prefer to buy from a friend, everything else being equal.

CHAPTER FIVE

The All-Important Inner You (IY)

CHAPTER FIVE

AS WE EMBARKED ON THIS CRAZY IDEA of writing a book we discussed the Inner You as it relates to marketing success. Ironically, in our youth, although we didn't know each other at the time, your humble authors discovered that we had each been strongly influenced by a highly acclaimed book written by Dr. Maxwell Maltz entitled Psycho-Cybernetics. For many years, Dr. Maltz had a flourishing practice as a reconstructive and cosmetic facial surgeon, lectured internationally on his medical specialty, and pursued a dual career as a prolific author. After a decade of counseling hundreds of patients and testing his evolving "success conditioning techniques" on athletes and marketers, he published his findings in the original Psycho-Cybernetics book. It was an instant best seller.

As a plastic surgeon Dr. Maltz observed that despite his best efforts and great surgical results, many patients' unhappiness and insecurities were not cured, as they *and* he believed would occur when he gave them the *perfect* new faces they desired. In his ground breaking book, he suggested that many people see themselves inaccurately, their perceptions distorted by the unchallenged and often erroneous beliefs imbedded in the subconscious mind. Ultimately, Dr. Maltz evolved from treating outer scars to treating inner scars.

Dr. Maltz went on to amass a wealth of "case history" material, seminars, workshops, radio broadcasts, over a dozen books all applying Psycho-Cybernetics to different purposes from business success to sex life improvement. In our book, we'll keep it to business success--- for sex life improvement, you're on your own!

We accept the work of Dr. Maltz and recommend his writings to you. We are particularly intrigued by how the Inner You (IY) projects outward through the Outer You (OY) to form your image to those around you. We believe that the IY can be altered in positive ways, that the benefits to you in happiness and success will be tremendous, and that they will cut across the full spectrum of your life. In this chapter we'll give you some specific things you can do to work on developing your IY.

First, it is important to be brutally honest with yourself in assessing your IY and coming up with goals for self improvement. Are you happy with yourself? Why or why not? Are you confident? Are you internally calm in trying times or do you become a basket case? Do you believe you are destined for success or do you feel you have a black cloud following you? Are you happy with your family relationships? Are you happy with your personal self-image? Why or why not? Do you feel a deep connection and commitment to your work? If not, why? Put your thoughts on paper. Write down the areas within your IY where you feel you're not flourishing. And, don't be hard on yourself because you do need improvement. We all do. It's just that some realize and admit it and others don't. The people who do realize their need for improvement are called *winners* because they are the ones who make progress. If you do your own self assessment you should reach over your shoulder and give yourself a huge pat on the back for being honest with yourself.

After honestly assessing your IY you'll have some areas for improvement. Since we don't know what they are and they're unique to you we can't give you the solutions but they should become apparent to you. We will tell you that **self-talk** is a very powerful way for you to reinforce any change you want to implement. *Visualize* the desired changes in your IY and develop a self-talk mantra to bring about the desired change. Repeat it regularly. After a while the new behavior or belief will become imbedded into your subconscious and you will automatically default to it.

We equate this to something we've witnessed in our own personal lives as youth baseball and basketball coaches… muscle memory. In sports there is a theory which states that a movement must be done about 1,000 times before it becomes "muscle memory" and becomes the subconscious way the body performs that movement. If a basketball player wants to change his free throw shooting technique he must shoot free throws the correct way about 1,000 times for it to become his natural way. The same goes for a baseball player who might be trying to change his swing.

Applying the "muscle memory" theory to changing an aspect of your IY will take patience on your part. It's hard to do something 1,000 times that doesn't come naturally. It would seem that 250, 500, or 700 would be enough. Patience isn't always a strong suit of the marketing personality but it is more easily brought about if one knows of the muscle memory theory and that it also applies to changing your IY. So, keep at it and take comfort in the knowledge that the "muscle memory" factor will kick in and it won't be as hard anymore. It'll just be the natural way you do things.

An interesting study conducted with mentally disturbed individuals showed that when they were told "act sane" for a period of two months they actually made significant progress and, in fact, did become saner. Just by "acting" sane! This begs the question as to what would happen if a marketer decided to "act" like a great marketer. We believe that said marketer would indeed become a better marketer. This is yet another way to effect a positive change in your IY. Whatever it is about your IY you want to change you can it, to a degree, just by "acting" like that's how you are. The human mind is truly an amazing thing and, if directed and followed, will lead you where you want to go. Through self analysis you can point your mind in the right direction and let it pull you to a higher level of achievement.

Great coaches in sports get the most out of their teams by placing individual players in game situations that minimizes what they don't do well while maximizing those things that they *do* perform well. You can be your own coach and do the same for yourself. Through better understanding of your strengths and weaknesses you can figure out ways to put yourself in a position to maximize the former while minimizing the latter. As the great philosopher Clint Eastwood said, "one must know one's limitations." If this means that you need to stop doing certain things in order to spend your time and energy in a more productive area, so be it. Don't worry about what you might be missing. As another, *truly* great philosopher said… "For everything you've missed, you've gained something else"--- Emerson.

Some people have extremely high altruistic tendencies. Their IY is filled with compassion and concern for others. Sometimes it is so much so that they neglect their own needs and desires. As with anything else there exists an entire spectrum if we were to measure levels of altruism. Mother Teresa would be a 10 on the scale while a very selfish person might be a 1. We believe that everyone can become more attuned to their altruistic side. We know that great marketers generally score very high on the altruism scale, like our friend German Vidal, the top Toyota salesman. And we know that the altruistic part of our being resides in our IY. And that the IY filters outward into how you are perceived by others, your image. So, it's important *and* smart to develop your altruistic side. Viewing it selfishly if you improve you compassion and concern for others you'll be a better marketer and make more money. Do you think German Vidal would get all of the referrals from happy customers if he weren't such a caring person?

So what do you do if you know you could be better? You'd like to be more caring and compassionate toward others but you've been the way you are for so long... how do you just flip a switch and change now? The answer is that there's no switch to flip. It's not that easy, but you *can* make some change. It does require changes in your routine and in your habits. We can't give you real specific things to do because you and your situation are unique. However, we can offer some general ways to begin a change. The first is to find an organization where you can volunteer to help others who are not as fortunate as you are. You can look on the internet at all kinds of organizations in your locale who are in need of volunteers. Maybe you want to work with troubled youth or go into nursing homes to brighten the day of our elderly. Whatever you choose, it should be something that exposes you to people or situations out of your current world. By doing this, you'll gain some new perspectives and it literally does change your thinking by expanding your ability to consider things from another perspective.

In the past decade we've seen a huge growth in "corporate caring." By this we mean the trend of companies and association sponsoring charity organizations. Sometimes they keep the same charity for a few years and other times the charity is a different one each year. Since marketers are leaders you may want to pick a charity and try to convince your company to raise funds for them. Taken a step further you can get involved in doing some type of physical volunteer work like cleaning up a park or a stretch of river. Then you could ask some of your customers to get involved with you. Just ask, don't push. Some will come along and you'll undoubtedly have a great bonding opportunity. Those who don't come will at least see you as a person who cares about others enough to give unselfishly of your time. So you really can't lose as long as you don't try to strong arm people into volunteering.

Developing the IY within you should be an ongoing process of personal growth whether you are a marketer or not. The fact that it will help you in your marketing career might be a lure to get you going but your reasoning for starting isn't as important as the fact that you do. You'll be a happier, more serene person ***and*** a better marketer.

Chapter Nuggets

Bet on yourself: Lay it all on the line, baby! Bet on yourself! Invest in your career by giving yourself the best training you can get. Supplement any company training with your own personal training program by doing things like studying MBD, taking seminars to hone your marketing skills, getting more product knowledge, or upgrading your customer profile software. The point is... don't skimp on yourself when it comes to giving yourself the tools for success.

Call Your Mother: Call your loved ones regularly just to see how they're doing. Our aging parents, aunts, uncles, grandparents all share that universal human need to connect with loved ones. Warm their hearts.

A lesson learned by watching Cal: We believe that the great ones in any field develop good habits and tend to do things the same way each time. One of your baseball loving authors, Island Boy, had season tickets to the Orioles during most of Cal Ripken's consecutive game streak. Arriving often well before the game, he was at the ball park early enough to watch the players warm up and stretch leisurely. Watching Cal's routine was fascinating. He'd go directly behind first base by about 5 feet and would stand on the right field foul line. He's run sprints to a spot in the outfield grass behind second base and back again. Before that though, he'd go through an elaborate stretching routine. He'd do it **exactly** the same way, in the same order before every game. Develop *your* good preparation habits and don't deviate unless it's a conscious change. What if Cal had skipped his stretching sometimes? Would Gehrig's record been broken? We think not. Don't take short cuts!

A smooth sea never made a great sailor: Appreciate your difficult times because without them you wouldn't develop to your full potential. We all need challenges in order to hone our skills. Difficult challenges often bring out positive sides and strengths people didn't know was within them. We tend to rise to the challenges placed before us.

Make an inner adjustment as you move between worlds: We believe in balance between our work and family. They are usually two separate and distinct worlds. Yet without harmony in one, the other is adversely affected. Therefore, we've found that a conscious effort to make an inner adjustment is a very helpful thing. For instance, say you've had a very busy, hectic day. Upon arriving home your kids excitedly run to you seeking your attention. Is your mind still in "workland?" We suggest a conscious inner adjustment, a switch in thinking just prior to entering your home. In your mind, take off your work hat. Put on your dad, mom, husband, or wife hat *before* you walk through the door. Practice this regularly and it will become habit. You'll likely reach a higher level of happiness in each of your worlds. And an emotionally balanced, well rounded individual makes a better marketer!

Visualize your competitor working hard: All of us have days when we need to kick our motivation level up a notch. None of us are superhuman. The next time you're having one of those days and don't have your "A" game, try this: Visualize a real or imagined competitor. Picture him or her somewhere out there having a great day, working hard, and doing all he/she can to cut into the business you've worked so hard to earn. Then make the most of the rest of **your** day! You can't control competitors but you *can* control what you do. Use your competitor to motivate yourself.

Be Humble: All of us have reasons to be humble. Even Babe Ruth struck out 1,300 times! Hopefully, all of us want to remain humble because it's the right way to live our lives. An added benefit is that most people want to do business with someone who is good at what they do yet humble about it. If you start feeling too impressed with yourself people get turned off. Step back every once in a while and make sure you keep your feet on the ground. It's always good to "remember where you came from."

Be a secret admirer: Choose someone in your field to model yourself after. You may have more than one. These should be people you personally know. Think about what makes them great at what they do and what you can learn from them.

Be patient: It usually takes longer than anticipated to break through to the sales level you want. Keep working hard. It'll come.

Focus on your own performance: The authors don't much believe in feeling a bunch of angst about what competitors may or may not be doing. We view it much like a good team in any sport approaches competition--- if we execute our game plan and do what we supposed to do then we'll probably be successful. We've never spent a lot of time researching competitors beyond the point of just generally knowing about their products and services. There are only so many hours in a day and you have a finite amount of energy. Save your energy for your very intense focus on winning customers, *not* researching competitors.

Refuse to give up: Things change with prospects. They become dissatisfied with the incumbent supplier of what you'd like to sell them or you've started to grow on them (you're building a relationship). For whatever reason it may be, things do change so hang in there. They'll admire your persistence and know that if they do give you their business you'll be around and won't bail out on them.

Harnessing Your Natural Creativity

CHAPTER SIX

WE ARE ALL BORN CREATIVE. Most of us just lose it somewhere along the way. We become socialized beings and learn where we fit in and what our various roles are. Our life and we ourselves become defined. We're doctors, lawyers, marketers, writers, grocery store managers, accountants, husbands, wives, sons, daughters, coaches, or a hundred other things. Stuff then is expected of us, and others look for us to stay somewhere within the prescribed norms of whatever our particular role might be. Conformity is the norm and is rewarded while our creativity is squelched. Our natural range of expression becomes limited. In many ways, this is a good thing. We shudder to think of a world full of only free spirited creative types. We need rigid, by the rules thinkers, to figure out how to build bridges and the other things marketers don't want to do. Of course, we need marketers to sell all of the materials used in building the bridge! All have a place in our great capitalistic system. We view it as a kind of ecosystem, like we learned about in high school biology, where every organism in the pond has a function and role.

The question here, for marketers is how to unlock your creative side or how to reverse-age yourself back to yesteryear when your creative side wasn't as stifled. To better understand how you can unleash your creativity let us first tell you about a man who has been called "the most creative person in the world." Although it is admittedly difficult to determine who really is the world's most creative person it'd be pretty hard to mount much of an argument against this individual. His name is Dr. Yoshiro Nakamatsu and he is a prolific Japanese inventor with over 2,300 patents to his credit--- more than double that of Thomas Edison who comes in second at 1,093. The next closest competitor holds a mere 400 patents. Among his inventions are the floppy disk which he sold to IBM, the compact disk, the compact disk player, the digital watch, and a water powered engine. As a marketer, we doubt you'll be trying to outdo the good Dr. N in the world of inventions but we discuss him to get into his methods and philosophy about how to make the most of the innate creativity within us. So, how exactly does he do it, what can we learn, and how can we apply these lessons in the everyday world of marketing?

A recent interview of Dr. Nakamatsu by author Chic Thompson provides a glimpse into the world of this remarkable man. Thompson himself is an inventor and creative type who wrote book entitled What a Great Idea and has a website by that name. Here are some excerpts from that interview:

Chic: So you feel that creativity comes from a balance of regimentation and freedom?

Nakamatsu: Yes, but freedom is most important of all. Genius lies in developing complete and perfect freedom within a human being. Only then can a person come up with the best ideas. (Hmmm…sounds like he's talking about the IY)

Chic: We have a difficult time in this country because we don't allow ourselves that kind of freedom. We have what we call the Protestant work ethic that says, "if at first you don't succeed, try and try again." To me, trying too hard stifles creativity.

Nakamatsu: That's unfortunate. It's crucial to be able to find the time and freedom to develop your best ideas.

Chic: Then tell me about your routine to spark creativity. I've heard that you come up with ideas underwater.

Nakamatsu: Yes, that's part of a three step process. When developing ideas, the first rule is you have to be calm. So, I've created what I call my "static" room. It's a place of peace and quiet. In this room, I have only natural things: a rock garden, natural running water, plants, a five-ton boulder from Kyoto. The walls are white. I can look out onto the Tokyo skyline, but in the room there is no metal, or concrete, only natural things like water and rock and wood.

Chic: So you go into your "static" room to meditate?

Nakamatsu: No, just the opposite. I go into the room to free-associate. It's what you must do before meditating, before focusing on one thing. I just throw out ideas-I let my mind wander where it will.

Chic: I call that "naïve incubation."

Nakamatsu: Yes, it's my time to let my mind be free. Then I go into my "dynamic" room, which is just the opposite of my "static" room. The "dynamic" room is dark, with black-and-white-striped walls, leather furniture, and special audio and video equipment. I've created speakers with between 12 and 40,000 hertz-which, you can imagine, are quite powerful. I start listening to jazz, then change it to what you call "easy listening," and always end with Beethovens Fifth Symphony. For me, Beethoven's Fifth is good music for conclusions.

Chic: And finally you go to your swimming pool...

Nakamatsu: Exactly-the final stage. I have a special way of holding my breath and swimming underwater-that's when I come up with my best ideas. I've created a Plexiglas writing pad so that I can stay underwater and record these ideas. I call it "creative swimming."

Chic: That seems to fit very well with the strategy I teach in my creativity workshops: discover and use your "idea friendly times."

Nakamatsu: Yes, but in doing this you must prepare your body. You can only eat the best foods. You cannot drink alcohol.

Chic: I've heard that you've come up with your own "brain food."

Nakamatsu: Yes, these are snacks I've invented, which I eat during the day. I've marketed them as Yummy Nutri Brain Food. They are very helpful to the brain's thinking process. They are a special mixture of dried shrimp, seaweed, cheese, yogurt, eel, eggs, beef, and chicken livers-all fortified with vitamins.

Later in the interview Nakamatsu addresses the need to be well rounded, eating right, and participating in the "right" athletics. He says: "A genius must be a well-rounded person, familiar with many things: art, music, science, sports. He or she can't be restricted to only one field of expertise." We believe strongly that this applies to marketers, who, in order to be interesting and dynamic need to be well versed in a wide range of topics. Interestingly, Nakamatsu contends that jogging, tennis, and golf are the "right" sports to spark creativity. Being baseball aficionados we were disappointed at our favorite sport not being included, especially since Dr, Nakamatsu played collegiate baseball... he was a pitcher. But who are we to question the "most creative person in the world?"

Why do we tell the story of Dr. Nakamatsu? Not because we expect you, Mr. and Ms. Marketer, to become inventors and rival his invention prowess. We merely want you to be better marketers, make lots of money, and have fun... modest, achievable goals. We relayed his story because we liked it and thought maybe it'll inspire you to get *your* creative juices going.

Obviously, it's not possible to will yourself to be creative. We do suggest a few things you can do to be more creative overall or more creative in a targeted way. First, you'll want to pick out your **creative cocoon**... the place you go to give incubate your ideas. It can be anywhere of your choosing but here is what to look for when picking out your *creative cocoon*: The best place is usually a serene, happy environment with neutral tones, minimalistic in design, and a very open feeling. The creative process cries out for calm and your *creative cocoon* should reflect that. So, now that you've got the place, think about a realistic schedule for your creative development. Pick days and times to give to this new important part of your marketing world.

Next, give thought to what you want to accomplish in your creative time. Do you want to come up with an idea to address a certain opportunity? Or do you only want to work on being more creative generically? Have an idea each time as to what it is you want to direct your creative energy toward. To accomplish this, do some preliminary thinking and preparation. For instance, we find it helpful to "surf the net" prior to going into a creative session. By "googling" your topic and spending a few minutes quickly scanning whatever comes up pertaining to it, you give fuel to the fires of your creative side. While in your creative session, focus loosely on your topic and let your mind wander over and around it. It is in this way that you'll generate the most ideas. Another trick of the creative trade is to always have a small notepad or recorder to jot down those elusive, but sometimes great thoughts that come at the oddest times. Re-visit later when you can give the idea your full attention. This also gives you something else to glance over to let other ideas "percolate." When you do actually get into your creative cocoon and into your creative session we suggest you not have a clock nearby at all but use a timer. Give yourself enough time so that you don't feel you're on some tight deadline… deadlines kill creativity. A method we like for honing creative abilities is to invent your own creative challenges. This is much like your own game show you can play out in your mind. Give yourself a challenge to come up with three ideas for a business you haven't seen before, or three new ways to market a product or service. Keep a journal of all of your sessions and review them periodically. After you've been doing this a while it's real interesting to re-visit some of your older creative thoughts and see how they might interplay with some of the newer ones. It becomes fun at this point and you'll be far more comfortable with the process. Before long you're well on your way to reaching the creative potential within you. Ideas, like money, should be viewed as your friend… they flow to you!

Chapter Nuggets

Make an artistic date with yourself: We got this nugget from Julia Cameron, author of *The Artist's Way*. She recommends setting aside a block of time each week to spend with the artist within. It is a time to nurture this side of you. Go to a museum, take a walk in nature, or see a matinee. This opens the creative door through which ideas and creativity enter. This works as well for marketers who want to enhance creativity as it does for artists.

Post goals on post-its in your house and car: Keep your goals in front of you. You might write a goal on a post-it and put it on your bathroom mirror. Or on the dashboard of your car. The more often you see the goal, the more imbedded in your brain it becomes.

Rent a dunking machine: If you have an event where this is at all possible rent one of the dunking machines you see at carnivals and county fairs. We're referring to the ones where the "dunkee" sits on a platform while contestants throw a ball at the target and the dunkee drops into the water when the target is hit. These are lots of fun and will give you and your customers something to talk and laugh about for years. Of course, *you* should be the one being dunked. You may even want to wear one of those old 1890s types of bathing suits in order to complete the look and really get into the role.

Split expenses for special events: If you want to pull off a special event for your customers but don't have enough money in the budget consider partnering with another quality company that serves the same market but doesn't compete with you.

Bring in lunch for customers/referral sources: It's always a hit when you take lunch into an office. What a nice way to say thanks! And, you may get to know them a little better over lunch.

Team up with other company reps: Find marketers from other companies who don't compete with you yet serve the same customer. Get to know these marketers and form alliances to refer each other. In Atlanta there is an organization of vendors who all sell to the insurance industry. Such vendors are premium finance companies, auto glass companies, restoration companies, and private investigator firms. They meet monthly and the marketers develop relationships and are able to help one another with referrals. Remember, they serve the same market but with different products and services so they aren't competing with one another. You don't need to join a formal organization to do this though. Some good nosing around on your part and you should be able to come up with a few marketers of other products who serve the same customer base that you do. Call them up and tell them how you might be able to help each other. You could meet with individuals or you could try to get a small group together.

Know when to let go: One of the biggest problems artists struggle with is when to stop working on a painting. Likewise, marketers sometimes will work on a mailing piece or marketing campaign far too long in an effort to get it just right. Sometimes, you've got to stop striving for perfection and say it is "good enough." The perfect marketing piece or campaign hasn't been written anyway! Often by letting go, the marketer finds that what they created indeed is "good enough" and the business begins to flow. Other times, letting go gives your marketing a chance to evolve through re-assessment.

Famous birthdays: Look up famous birthdays and think of ways to tie them into your business. For instance, on Einstein's birthday you might send a card with Einstein's photo and write in: "We've got a genius of a deal."

Ask for forty-seven seconds of phone time when calling for an appointment: When you're calling someone to schedule a presentation, tell them immediately that you only need forty-seven seconds of their time on the phone. Then stick to your word… cut to the chase and schedule that face to face meeting. This works!

Send birthday cards: We've been amazed at how this simple thing is so effective, especially if it's a card just for them with a handwritten note—as opposed to those stupid cards you buy in packs of 100 and are the birthday card equivalent of a form letter. We've had people tell us how much our cards have meant and sometimes we've been the only non-family members sending cards to our customers.

MBD Communication - AKA Delightful Dialogue

CHAPTER SEVEN

COMMUNICATING EFFECTIVELY IS A KEY TO SUCCESS for any marketer, in every industry. Communication involves so much more than mere words spoken or written. Presentation, body language, tonal qualities, facial expressions, context, and timing are but a few of the factors coming into play.

We had the good fortune to meet someone who has authored twelve books on effective communications and related topics. His name is Morey Stettner and we met him shortly after he wrote his first book entitled, *The Art of Winning Conversation.*

Stettner tells us there should be *three* distinct stages to your approach: **Prepare** thoroughly for any persuasive encounter, **listen** raptly, and then **speak** with clarity and passion using a mix of questions and power phrases (action words). We shorten Stettner's three stages to **PLS**. This process is simple and direct, yet so elegant that with practice it will become second nature. In the preparation stage it is important to note that you'll need an unshakable belief in your ability to sway opinion or change minds. During the preparation stage you'll want to identify your customer's hot buttons so that you can push them later. Then you'll want to rehearse which we'll discuss later. In the listening stage remember that listening is not as easy as it seems but you have to do it well or be doomed to mediocrity. Why is it so important to be a good listener? It's simple… it makes the other person feel important. And we learn more about them. Everyone yearns to be heard, and to feel that others care about what they say. The speaking stage is an outgrowth of detailed preparation and careful listening. Stettner maintains, and we concur that all three stages—**preparing, listening,** *and* **speaking (PLS)**—blend together to maximize your communication power.

Stettner suggests a great way to listen effectively when talking with either of the two extremes of conversationalists—the incessant babbler or the slow, boring speaker. In each case, he suggests you use what he calls a "one word tag." For instance, if a babbler is complaining about his unpleasant experience in a clothing store you might boil it all down to three tag words… price, rudeness, and selection. Come up with these tag words as he is droning on. Then, you are able to repeat back to him: "So, Joe, you feel you paid too much, weren't treated well, and they had little to choose from." Joe would then know that you had listened. You might have been tempted to let your mind wander and not get what he was saying had you not used the *tag word technique*. It works just as well for the slow talker who bores you to tears. Try this. It's an awesome tool to have in your repertoire.

As a marketer, you will undoubtedly have opportunities to speak in front of groups of varying sizes. Whether speaking to a group of 2,200, or 2,000 all of us experience nervousness. It's natural and normal. Great speakers are no different than you—the have just developed coping strategies to get their nerves working for them rather than against them. Along with an attack of nerves comes adrenaline, which *can* be an advantage because when harnessed adrenaline comes out in the form of passion and enthusiasm… a desired result. We've discovered a secret way to beat the nerves by doing a psych job on yourself prior to your speaking engagement. Tell yourself how much **fun** it's going to be to speak to that particular group. In your mind, tell yourself how lucky you are that you **get** to do this. Think about the difference in feeling that you **want** to do something as opposed to **having** to do something. We guarantee that if you go into your presentation feeling, "Oh no, I have to give this presentation," you won't be at your best. Just remind yourself how lucky you are to have such this great opportunity. After a few times trying this approach you'll become a believer!

We also recommend bonding with your audience immediately prior to your presentation if this is at all possible. Great speakers almost always mingle with their audiences prior to speaking. Introduce yourself to as many individuals as you can. Give them a warm smile and make them feel you're exactly where you want to be and that you're looking forward to being able to spend time with them. Be sure to shake hands—never underestimate the value of physical touch. It'll be a lot harder for your audience to give you a difficult time if you've "made friends" with them right before you go on. This "trick of the trade" is widely taught in professional speaker training because it's so effective.

There's an old maxim in the presentation business that says a speaker should *tell the audience what he's going to tell them, then tell them, and then tell them what he just told them.* We recommend that you use this technique. And always add a **call for action** at the end of a persuasive presentation.

Whether speaking to a group or to an individual try to be succinct. Your words will be much better received if you cut to the chase. Meaningless extra words increase the likelihood of your message getting tuned out.

We've found that organizing your thoughts and words into *groups of three* is a way to increase retention. Multiple studies have found the human mind seems to remember things well when grouped in threes. This is thought to be because we associate them together, making it more likely to recall them all individually. If you look throughout our book you'll find many groupings of three when we are attempting to make a point—this is by design. Three word phrases tend to have more power because they inherently get right to the point. Consider the following: "I'll be there." "I appreciate you." "Maybe you're right." "Just do it." These phrases when spoken within their contexts leave no doubt or room for misinterpretation. And their power is palpable when combined with good eye contact and body language. Sometimes, you'll find separating three items or thoughts by commas is effective. For instance, are you "ready, willing, and able" to help? Do you remember what Superman fought for? It was "truth, justice, and the American Way." Flags of nations are often in three colors, as in the "red, white, and blue." Start to think in threes when *preparing for presentations, writing copy,* or *talking one-on-one.* Even the previous sentence is a "three" sentence—see how it works? Confucius spoke in threes saying... "There are three marks of a superior man: being virtuous, he is free from anxiety; being wise, he is free from perplexity; being brave, he is free from fear."

To communicate well you have to rehearse! Great marketing and great communication requires hard work. If it were easy, anybody could do it, right? Rehearsing *is* work and isn't always what you want to be doing but we're here to tell you that there is no short cut. Let your competitor skip this step but you'd better not. By the time you finish this book we hope you'll forever be an MBD marketer and no self-respecting MBD devotee would go on stage without rehearsing. You can do this in the car, in the shower, or just about anywhere. Do rehearse, but do NOT memorize! Know your material in a broad, general sense and you'll find your presentations will be much more natural sounding, relaxed, and you'll seem in better command of your subject matter. We do suggest writing several bullet points visible to you during your talk. These bullet points should be one word only but each word should remind you of a large topic upon which you can expand extemporaneously. This makes for a good "safety net" so that you won't worry about forgetting your major points.

We haven't addressed your speaking voice yet but that too, is an important element in the communication package. The voice should be viewed as an instrument or tool, and in the MBD world being aware of how to use your voice may give you an edge. First, let's acknowledge and accept that *everyone* thinks their own recorded voice sounds weird. So, just forget about using that as an excuse not to work on using your voice more effectively. Nor should you resign yourself to accepting whatever characterization you might put on your voice—too monotone, too high–pitched, whatever. Experiment with your voice, especially when rehearsing a presentation. Record yourself and listen to the replay. Try to vary the intensity and tonal quality of your voice to command attention at the times of your choosing—when you want to drive home a persuasive point, for example. Also, work on varying the pitch of your voice because this helps the listener pay attention. You can also experiment with differing paces when making presentations. For instance, you might want to adopt a slower, thoughtful appearing presentation for some groups and situations. Other times might call for a quick, passionate presentation. It's always an advantage if you can become flexible in this regard and adjust your presentation to fit each situation. As always though, be patient with yourself and don't be discouraged if you have mixed results while trying these new things. It's just like learning to field ground balls for young, inexperienced baseball players—you'll miss a bunch and make errors but you will improve if only you don't give up!

Your competitors are likely not consciously working to improve their communication skills. This is an overlooked area by most marketers. Most accept their communicative skill level as what it is, as though it is something beyond their control. We say it's just like anything else... practice brings improvement! Improvement brings more money!

Chapter Nuggets

Join Toastmasters: This is the best, most fun way to improve your performance and comfort level with public speaking. Toastmasters is a great organization and has helped thousands improve their public speaking skills. This doesn't have to mean speaking in front of hundreds from a fancy podium. You might need to get better at doing presentations to groups of four to ten people and Toastmasters might be just the thing for you. You can visit a local chapter as a guest to observe the format.

Allow customers a bad day: We all have bad days. Maybe our spouses fussed at us, maybe we're having trouble with our kids, or maybe we're dealing with health problems. If your customer seems to be having a bad day, isn't as pleasant as normal, or appears inexplicably grumpy give them a break. Tell yourself not to take it personally. Assume they've had something negative occur which has caused them to be in a funk. Assume it's a blip on the screen and they'll be back to their normal self next time. Isn't this how you'd want others to view *your* bad days?

Have a phone phenom in your office: Every office needs a go-to person to handle delicate or difficult phone calls, those conversations with customers who are frustrated, impatient, or angry. We used to work with a young woman by the name of Rebecca Joyce. Rebecca was knowledgeable about our business but more importantly, she knew how to talk with customers. Notice we say talk "with" not at customers. It helps that Rebecca had a lovely, proper British accent and a voice that was easy on the ears. And she was patient. She was the person we always went to when we needed to put forth our most empathetic, compassionate face. Every office needs a Rebecca. If you don't have one, find one. You may have someone who fits the bill already working at your company. Identify them as your go-to person and present it as an honor bestowed upon them. It *is*. It's a recognition of their communication skills.

Think twice before entertaining two or three clients: It's usually not a good idea to entertain two or three customers at one time. It's better to entertain one or many. When trying to divide your time and attention between two or three people it is inevitable that at least one will feel the odd man out. And, face it, you'll probably have a favorite and it will be hard to keep that hidden. Even if you try, body language and other subtle non-verbal cues may betray you.

Put your Web address on everything: Web marketing is hugely important so be sure to use it whenever you can. And *tell* customers to check you out on the Web.

Call customers by name when you pick up phone: No, we don't expect you to be psychic. When the customer calls to speak to someone at your office and the phone answerer learns their name she/he transfers the call and tells the person getting the call who is calling for them. Then that person can pick up the phone and cheerfully greet the person by name instead of the usual, "may I help you?" This tells the caller that the first person cared enough to relay who is calling and makes a good first impression.

Carry thank you notes like Princess Di did: Princess Di had a habit of carrying royal thank you notes with her at all times. After spending time with someone she'd put the person's name and address on the envelope when she got back to her limo. Now you may not have a limo yet but the point is that Lady Di was prepared and wanted to make sure she didn't forget… a good lesson for all of us. A handwritten note says to the recipient that you spent extra time thinking of them and went to extra effort. And that says a lot a lot about you.

Don't be honest with them: How often have you heard a marketer use the phrase… to be honest with you? As opposed to what? Being dishonest? Saying "to be honest with you" sounds as though you usually aren't honest. Just make your statement and let it stand on its own.

Silence can be an ally: All too often marketers want to rush in to fill gaps of silence. Resist this temptation. View the silence as an ally. You'll learn more about your customer as they rush to fill the gap. This also helps you persuade them because you'll be more likely to flush out objections.

Give genuine, warm greetings: The glow of one warm thought is worth more to me than money—Thomas Jefferson.

"And" beats but: When summarizing what someone says don't say, "yes, but" if you disagree. Instead, use, "yes, and I think. For instance, "You say that a 55 mph speed limit makes sense, and I think…" is better than saying, "You say that a 55 mph speed limit makes sense *but* I think."

Develop a fifteen-second story: If you don't tell your story and frame it as you want, who will? If you don't brag on the benefits you offer (while appearing humble), who will? If you come up with a fifteen second pitch that succinctly captures who you are, what you do, and how it will help your customer you will be *amazed* at the results. For instance, an AFLAC insurance representative sells policies to individuals through their employer. AFLAC provides a check paid directly to the individual if they are treated for cancer. Mr. AFLAC marketer puts it this way: "I'm the guy who gives you cash, over and above health insurance, no questions asked, if you are treated for cancer." Bingo—inless than fifteen seconds the prospect understands the benefit. A stockbroker might say, "we help people build wealth $100 at a time." A mobile auto detailer could say, "I bring auto detailing to you so that you can keep working." Have fun with your fifteen second stories. Change them as makes sense. They are great to use at networking meetings, like BNI, where each person gets to stand up and say something very brief about what it is they do.

E-mail-land is danger zone: Beware the Big M…misinterpretation. E-mail has no facial expression or tone of voice, which leaves way too much leeway for the receiver to factor in his own interpretation. Re-read your e-mails before hitting the send button. Ask yourself if it could possibly be taken another way… one that you don't intend. Or, worse yet, that could damage you. If you see a possible problem a little re-wording will be time well spent.

Keep up on news in the sports world: You may not even like sports and that's fine. But the fact is that most Americans do. Like the weather, sports are one of the most talked about subjects of all. If you are oblivious to sports altogether you'll be excluded from bonding opportunities. We mean that you need to at least know whether the popular local teams are having a great season, a poor season, and generally be aware of what's going on. Just read the sports page two or three times a week and you'll be good to go!

Improve your listening skills: This is a hard thing to do. Our minds tend to wander. Sometimes we're thinking about what we're going to say next as our customer talks. Other times rather than maintaining good eye contact we're distracted by something else in our field of vision. We've all had the experience of talking with someone only to have them looking around over our shoulder to whoever or whatever is lurking there. It's pretty irritating and it happens all the time. Great listeners are few and far between because it *is* so hard to do. But that's good for you—if everyone was already a great listener it'd be that much harder for you to stand out. Focus on the speaker as completely as you can. Give him/her ALL of your attention. Think about people in your life you are good listeners and think about how they position their bodies to receive what you're saying. Usually they will face you squarely with good eye contact and an interested expression. This really shouldn't be hard to do but it is. It requires a lot of determination.

Make use of the back of your business card: Most people only use 50% of their business card! In this case, we believe in the old adage, "the more you tell, the more you sell." Most people waste the space on the back of their cards. Why? It's perfectly good space and accepts ink just as readily as the front. And it gives you more to say when handing it out. When giving out your card always refer people to the back to read whatever bit of brilliance you've put there. A chiropractor we know puts his office hours on the back. Ask yourself what more you'd like to say that you didn't have room for on the front. Or try to think of a provocative question or surprising fact that would increase interest in your product or service. This one is easy, folks. Use ALL of your business card. Think of the back as a billboard.

Minimize paperwork: Do your best to keep paperwork to a minimum. It's so easy for valuable marketing hours being squandered by unnecessary paperwork burdens. You're a marketer, not an office clerk! If you spending too much time doing paperwork try to implement some changes.

Be a maniac about returning calls promptly: So many people in business today are not very good at returning calls promptly. You can be a star just by doing what you're supposed to do. Call people back right away and you'll be amazed at the compliments you'll get.

Repeat yourself: The fact that you've told your customer about your other services doesn't mean they'll remember. In the information age we live in a person has enough of a challenge remembering all they need to about their own business, much less yours. So, keep telling them.

Send "I'm pulling for you cards": Send this when someone is going for an exam or is trying to overcome something

The Awesome Power of Props

CHAPTER EIGHT

YOUR AUTHORS DISCOVERED EARLY IN OUR CAREERS about the power of using props in presentations and how this technique can gain customer attention quicker and increase the chances for marketing success. We learned that customer enthusiasm about our products and services didn't always match ours. At times, in our inexperience, we foolishly expected the prospect to be just as jacked up about our fabulous company as we were. We wrongly expected them to quickly understand and appreciate the features and benefits of our product. We soon learned that the discrepancy between the marketer and customer perspective is perfectly normal. Sometimes the customer really doesn't care about our product or service. They believe they are already using something better that meets their needs or is at least equal to our offering. In those early days, we'd go charging into our sales call thinking the prospect was dying to hear our pitch and would be hanging on every utterance coming from our flapping gums. In reality, our prospects were often thinking something like, "Ho, hum, here we go again. Here comes another marketing person who's going to make all kinds of claims about how great they are."

Remember too, that when we as marketers waltz into our customer's office we have no idea what has been going on in their business or personal life. We tend to think that just because they've agreed to see us that they are eager to hear our presentation. Here are just a few things that may have occurred in your prospects life just before you walked into their office: They just left a stressful meeting with their boss. They just got off the phone with an irate customer. They just had a meeting with an unhappy employee. They have ten phone messages on their desk from people awaiting return calls. They just got a call from school telling them their child got into trouble today. They had a fight with their spouse. They just got a promotion. This is the last day before their vacation starts and they are swamped with work as they try to get out of town. We could go on and on with this list but you get the point. Your prospects and customers have a lot of things going on and you can't just expect to prance into their office and command their undivided attention. Fortunately, we do have a solution that can help you deal with this ever-present challenge. What's this solution? Using **props** to grab and keep their attention. And educate them.

So, what's a prop? A prop as we define it in the MBD world is any physical item the prospect/customer can see, feel, touch, hear, or smell that a marketer can use in his presentation. One of your authors, Coach Bruce, has used props in a lot of selling situations in different industries. Early on in his marketing career, Coach Bruce sold pharmaceuticals to physicians. The primary responsibility of a pharmaceutical sales rep is to persuade the physician to prescribe more of his/her company's products. Sometimes the product is an old one and the physician has his mind made up about the product. The good doctor had already decided how and under which medical conditions he/she would use it. Coach Bruce's job was to get the doctor to prescribe his products for a wider range of maladies when he suspected the doctor was using it in a limited way. We're sure our readers will like Coach Bruce's creative MBD style solution, even in those early pre-MBD years. The product he happened to be selling was a bulk laxative—no jokes please—a product that had been on the market for more than thirty years. Clearly, this was a mature product that physicians knew a lot about. The obvious problem is how to get the physician to listen to a presentation on a product that's thirty years old. Coach Bruce's creative side came up with a prop, and like the product, the prop is nothing new. In fact, he chose the lowly roll of toilet paper to be his prop to garner the attention of the good doctor. He laid that roll of toilet paper right on that physician's desk. *Immediately*, he had his attention! The physician looked at the toilet paper, looked at Coach Bruce, and smiled—clearly wondering what was coming next. What was next was a well prepared, succinct presentation to an attentive customer. And, yes—it worked. The doctors prescribed more! Another prop he used when presenting to doctors was a simple safety valve from a tubeless tire. We'll spare you the lengthy explanation, but Coach Bruce was able to make a sales point involving a medical procedure that could be illustrated by the safety valve. In yet another situation in the medical field he used a child's toy, Dumbo the elephant scale, to demonstrate a concept to a small group of physicians and it worked in helping to command their attention on a topic about which they thought they already knew it all. The above examples have the goal to get the customer's attention focused on you. Obviously, you have to pivot to a crisp, clear presentation once you grab their attention. In other situations props may fall into the educational rather than attention getting area. We've given numerous seminars to insurance agents while we were in the water damage restoration business. Usually, these agents attend the seminars because we provided four hours of continuing education credits, which they must have in order to renew their insurance license. They'd usually come expecting to be bored but we usually far exceeded their expectations because we made it fun.

The fact that we had them at the Outback Steakhouse and included a free lunch helped too. In this setting we used props comprised of instruments used in the water damage restoration business such as moisture meters, infrared cameras, and dehumidification equipment. We also brought some examples of moldy carpeting we'd taken out of homes where the homeowner did not have their water damage situation addressed properly. In their seminar evaluations, many attendees told us how much they learned by being able to actually see how some of the equipment worked.

We suggest you consider how you might be able to use props in your marketing calls and presentations. Remember, they can be of the attention focusing variety, the educational, or both. Are there some props you can think of that will help your customer understand your product or service better? Try to come up with a least five props that you might be able to use. You'll discover that using props is fun and will liven up your day as well as your customers. Have fun with it but realize it's a serious money making enhancer!

Chapter Nuggets

Have a plaque made of articles featuring your customer: If you see a favorable newspaper or magazine article featuring your customer take it to a trophy shop. They can put the article onto a beautiful wooden plaque. This is *always* a big delight!

Be proud or be gone: If you aren't proud of your company, and what you do find something else that you *can* feel proud of and passionate about. Your chances of attaining financial success are *far* greater when you love, or are at least proud of what you're doing.

Make friends, sales follow: Make friends with people. Most prefer to buy from a friend, everything else being equal.

Always be positive…i.e., never tell someone they look tired: Think about it—Is anyone ever going to feel anything positive from hearing that they look tired? Only say things that make your customer feel better about themselves.

Our Very Own MBD Plan ¿ YOUR Very Own MBD Plan

CHAPTER NINE

WE'VE GIVEN YOU A LOT OF INFORMATION in this book. That was our intent. We're just a couple of wild and crazy guys who had a lot to say and thought we could write a book. So, here we are. We wrote it. You read it. Where do we all go from here?

Okay, we'll answer the preceding question first. We're planning to develop the MBD concept further because we know we can help and inspire marketers. Yeah, we hope to make a few bucks along the way but, hey we gotta eat too! We want to bring interested marketers together to bring out the best in each other at our workshops. We'll also have some great offerings and other cool stuff on our web site. Our dream is to have you guys, out there in reader-land, to write to us in droves. We want you to tell us of your MBD experiences, even if they were before you knew the MBD label. We'll figure a way to weave the good stories into our next venture. It's a cool thing to share your good ideas with your marketing brothers and sisters. We all feed off of and inspire each other.

We told you our plans. So where do **you** go from here? There are so many ideas in this book. Which ones should you use? We have a suggestion to figure it out. Here's how to formulate your own MBD marketing:

1. Go back through each chapter. Spend five minutes skimming the chapter and make a list of things/ideas you might be able to use. Do this for each chapter, including this one.

2. After doing step 1 put it all aside for 24 hours. Don't look at it.

3. Between 24 and 36 hours pick it up again and re-read the list you made. Look at what you chose from each chapter and how they interrelate and look for ways to use the ideas singly or together. Ideas

should flow. Write them down as fast as they come. Take your time with this stage.

4. Now, the contemplative stage. You have to give it all some time to soak in. Give yourself some time to plan the changes you'll want to make from the things you've learned or re-discovered while reading MBD.

5. Play your plan. Notice we didn't say work your plan. It should be play. If you get anything out of this book get this—have fun! Put your plans into play and play your plans. Think about that one.

6. Re-Think your MBD plan every couple of months. Skim the book again. There are lots of good ideas. Remember too, that your work environment is ever changing. Therefore, what works today might not in two months and vice versa. Revisit ideas to see if they're a better fit with your current situation.

We have to admit that it's a pretty cool feeling to finish our first book, which was long held dream of ours. If a couple of knuckleheads like us can write a book you guys, our beloved readers, should be able to come up with unbelievable MBD marketing plans! Go out there and have fun with all this!

We'll leave you with some wise words written in 1912 by Christian D. Larsen that was originally published in a book titled *Your Forces and How to Use Them.* Optimist International adopted his words as their official creed in 1922. The author was a prolific writer and lecturer who believed that people have tremendous latent powers, which could be harnessed for success with the proper attitude. We could think of no better way to end our book than with his words, The Optimist Creed. Aspire to these goals and you'll soar:

The Optimist Creed

To be so strong that nothing can disturb your peace of mind.

To talk health, happiness, and prosperity to every person you meet.

To make all your friends feel there is something worthwhile in them.

To look at the sunny side of everything and make your optimism come true

To think only of the best, to work only for the best, and to expect only the best.

To be just as enthusiastic about the success of others as you are about your own.

To forget the mistakes of the past and press on to the greater achievements of the future.

To wear a cheerful countenance at all times and give a smile to every living creature you meet.

To give so much time improving yourself that you have no time to criticize others.

To be too large for worry, too noble for anger, too strong for fear, and too happy to permit the presence of trouble.

Thanks for reading our book. We hope you it takes you to the next level. May the lessons you learned in **Marketing by Delight** bring you a mother lode of gold!

LaVergne, TN USA
19 November 2009
164664LV00003B/43/A